Dedicated to B.D. O'M for teaching me how to read and

write

&

To W.L. N in supporting all of my endeavors in a life of

partnership.

The Federal Reserve Bank, Treasury, Income Taxes and Debt: Connecting the Dots?

Preface

To casual observers of the Fed – as it became known – the very word "federal" conveys a governmental, public aspect to the system. If one does a Google search for "federal reserve system" the first site that comes up is www.federalreserve.gov.

In "About the Fed" Five faces appear: Ben Bernanke, Donald Kohn, Kevin Warsh, Elizabeth Duke and Daniel Tarullo. These five are members of the board. These members as far as the media reports are "independent" of the banking system. Of course this could be no further from the truth.

They are in fact selected!

To the casual observer, surely dot-gov. refers to government run institution?

This is not the case. It is a private institution masquerading as a 'federal' entity or government run institution.

The Fed actually lends money to the banks at interest determined by the discount rate and ensures that each bank maintains required reserves ratios dictated by the Fed. In turn the banks lend over night to their peers at the Fed funds rate to ensure that each bank maintains required reserve ratios, i.e. ration between deposits held in the bank and loans outstanding externally lent by the bank.

And as we continue to print money from the Treasury, the idea that the Fed is a government run institution could be no further from the truth.

It is in fact a private institution run by the main banks and has been such since the very beginning, back in 1913.

The purpose of this book is to explain in plain language exactly what the Fed does, is supposed to do and how it was formed.

Further how the US Treasury collects taxes through the IRS and spends those taxes? And finally how US national debt is issued, who owns it and who is responsible for its repayment?

As a student of economics and business in Ireland and then an adjunct professor of business, I was always mystified by what the Fed (and Central banks in general) actually did and why it was formed.

Many students over the years have asked me the following questions: "What does the Fed actually do? Does it print money? Is it a government run entity? Is it run privately?" Many conventional text books answer these questions in the usually bland and rote way, explaining the reality in a paltry manner.

It is my mission in this book to present the facts and supporting evidence on the gradual creep of power of the Fed in tandem with the United States Treasury and how these two entities have been responsible for boom-bust economic cycles since 1913. In fact it was for this precise reason that the Fed was set up: to avoid the boom-bust model. Each boom and bust results in massive transfers of wealth from one group in society to another group, mostly guaranteed by the taxpayer and facilitated by the government via the Fed/Treasury duo.

To all of those students and non-students alike, this book is for you. For all who are really interested in how the monetary system works this is your book. To all ordinary Americans who care about how this country is being run and its future, this book is for you.

Finally to the generations of children born and yet to be born, who most likely will inherit the massive debt burden that has been hoisted upon your shoulders, without your consent, this is for you!

A. P. O'Malley, November 2011, New York City

Table of Contents

Chapter 1

In The Beginning: There Was... No Income Tax!

What backs up a country's currency?

In economics we are taught that a currency is backed up by its exports, the more it exports, the more demand for that currency. So logically if a country has a massive balance of trade, and therefore a surplus, other countries will demand more of that country's currency.

The reality however is not as the theory goes.

The United States has trade deficits with almost every country in the world and of 196 countries that trade within the global system, the US is dead last at 196th.

If this is the case why then is the US Dollar king?

The answer to this has its roots in the seedlings that were planted in 1913.
In 1913 two major changes occurred in the United States of America.

The first was the creation of income tax and the second was the formation of the Federal Reserve Bank a system.

Two controversial laws were passed, both in that year.

The first act had its roots in the 16th Amendment which was ratified by Congress on February 3rd 1913 and was the basis for the Federal Income Tax Act or Revenue Act of 1913. In 1914 income tax rates were between 1% ($0 to $20,000) and 7% (over $500,000), increasing to 2%, 3%, 4%, 5% and 6% depending on annual income.

The second was passed on December 23rd 1913, just before Christmas. The Federal Reserve Act came into being by the stroke of Woodrow Wilson's pen. According to the Fed's website this act struck a "balance between the competing interests of private banks and populist sentiment".

The Federal Reserve System was based in twelve regions throughout the US. These regions were as follows: Richmond, Philadelphia, Boston and New York City in the east, San Francisco in the west, Minneapolis, Chicago, St. Louis, Cleveland and Kansas in the mid-west and Dallas and Atlanta in the south, making a total of twelve.

Curiously the US capital, Washington DC has no Federal Bank, but does house the board.

Each of these regions was assigned district numbers, with Boston at number one, New York two, Cleveland three and so on across the country to district twelve on the west coast.

The question that I hope to answer here is whether it was a coincidence that a full eleven months after this act was signed into law, the Federal Reserve Act was passed, or that it was engineered that way?

This question is of the utmost importance, since the ability of the Fed to issue currency was now based on the ability of the Congress to tax the people directly. And this allowed the Treasury to collect those taxes and issue debt on the basis of those taxes collected, since US government debt, which is over $14,000,000,000,000 (yes that's twelve zeros) has to be paid off every time a US government bond matures.

In the following chapter I will discuss how this issuance of debt is related to taxes.

Chapter 2

Issuance of Debt into Perpetuity

As the government, through the Treasury issues bonds the ability of the US to pay these off is based on taxes collected. The more taxes available to the government, the further into perpetuity the government can issue debt, through a bond. There are several types of US government bonds or treasuries. There are also notes.

I will concentrate on the medium to long term bonds and notes, since they are a better indicator of interest rates.

First we have the daddy of them all – 30 year treasury. These are issued in denominations ranging from $1000 to $1,000,000. The US Treasury curiously no longer issues 30 years, but they can be purchased on the secondary markets.

The 30 year bond is followed by the 10, 5, 3 and 2 year note. All of these are issued directly by the US Treasury and are sold at public auction.

How does it all work? The bond holder lends money to the US government and is guaranteed an interest rate over the life of the bond, collecting the original principal and that interest upon maturity. For example in 1980 a 30 year bond purchased in November of that year, was yielding a whopping (1) 12.4%, compounded over time.

---

1. *This according to the St. Louis Federal Reserve* [http://research.stlouisfed.org/fred2/data/GS30.txt]

These bonds comes due, maturing in November of 2010 and have to be repaid to those who purchased them. If a bond was bought in November 1999, it yielded just 6.15%, one half of what the 1980 bond was yielding. This 1999 bond will come due in November 2029 and so on and so forth.

So in simple terms once the bond becomes due the government must come up with money to repay the bondholder.

From where does the government get this money? Through the Treasury which is the parent of the often unruly IRS.

The Treasury has tasked the IRS with collecting the majority of taxes from private citizens, corporations and small to medium sized businesses.

In 2008 for example personal taxation from citizens made up 45% of total tax collections.

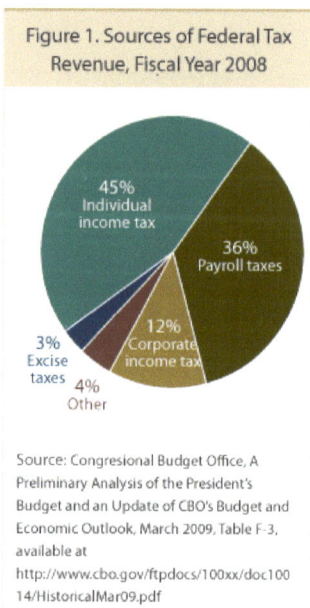

Figure 1. Sources of Federal Tax Revenue, Fiscal Year 2008

Source: Congresional Budget Office, A Preliminary Analysis of the President's Budget and an Update of CBO's Budget and Economic Outlook, March 2009, Table F-3, available at http://www.cbo.gov/ftpdocs/100xx/doc100 14/HistoricalMar09.pdf

According to the Tax Policy Center (previous chart) reported taxes collected by the IRS in 2008 amounted to $2.5 Trillion (or 17.7% of GDP). The Tax Policy Center also offered this nugget of information: "individual income tax has been the largest source of federal revenue since 1950, averaging just 8% of GDP."

The pie chart above yields another golden egg of information: corporate taxes accounted for just 12% of total tax take and according to the Tax Policy Center: "revenue from corporate income tax fell from between 5 to 6% in the early 1950s to 2.1% in 2008."

This is a paltry amount when compared to the individual taxpayer. Check out the basic math:

45% of $2,500,000,000,000 = $1,125,000,000,000
2.1% of $2,500,000,000,000 = $52,500,000,000

In other words corporations paid 2.1/45 times less than ordinary citizens in 2008.

That's 21.428571 times less as a percentage of GDP. Or $52.5 billion versus $1.125 trillion! Incidentally the .428571 recurs into infinity just as the government's ability to tax the individual recurs into perpetuity! In this book I'm concerned only with the three main sources of government revenue: corporate, payroll and individual income taxes (W-2 income).

The chart shows 12%, 36% and 45% respectively.

In 2008, payroll taxes were three times more a contributor to total tax take than corporate taxes.

Payroll taxes include taxes collected by employers of small businesses on behalf of their employees. Small to medium sized businesses are the biggest creator of jobs in the United States of America, but yet are burdened with 3 times more taxes than corporations (which are downsizing and off shoring jobs annually).

The table above shows how small businesses and entrepreneurs are dynamic engines of the trio: growth, generated taxation and job creation.

Chapter 3

Banking As We Knew It

Depository institutions such as banks and credit unions used to be fiscally responsible and executed their fiduciary duty with great care.

A customer deposited hard earned income, maintained a savings account and received interest on that amount annually. The bank in turn lent out that deposit at a slightly higher rate and profited from the spread.

This was the classic idea behind banking.

All of this changed with the dismantling of the Glass-Steagall Act (GSA) which had been passed in the wake of the financial crash of October 29th, 1929. It was passed in 1933 to ensure that the financial markets and institutions would never again be exposed to massive implosion. It separated the activities of commercial and investment banks. It was followed later in 1933 and 1934 by an act that established the SEC.

By November 12th 1999, just 66 years later, Glass-Steagall was dead and buried, repealed by an ex-governor of Arkansas and new president William J. Clinton.

The Gramm Leach Bliley Act (GLBA) replaced it and was heralded at the time as being: "legislation allowing" financial institutions "the freedom to innovate in the new economy." 90% of Congress overwhelmingly voted for the act with (1) 79 votes and a paltry voting 7 against it.

Under GSA, depository banks were required by law to be more fiscally conservative and less risk oriented, thus protecting the deposits of those ordinary people who saved with banks. The GLBA sent a message to the banks that they were free to do whatever they liked now that Clinton had taken over the reigns of the economic stallion.

And that stallion was ready to run riot all over the place.

With the internet taking hold and Greenspan keeping interest rates as low as possible, the economy began to run into the home straight.

Now the big depository banks like JP Morgan Chase, Citibank and others were allowed to engage in all kinds of activities from underwriting stock offerings to selling life insurance and issuing complicated derivatives to anyone or any financial institution that would buy them. Imagine a bank with billions of dollars in deposits now engaging in all kinds of Las Vegas casino speculation?

This was precisely what happened in the late nineties and early 2000s.

Exactly seventy years from the 1929 crash, the big banks had free reign again. And the characters involved in the dismantling of GSA would be the very same ones that would come begging the Congress ten years later for bail out assistance: Citibank, JP Morgan Chase, Wells Fargo et al. Under current rules commercial banks must fulfill a reserve requirement of 10%. In other words, they must keep 10% of deposits inside the bank but are allowed to lend out the other 90%. Imagine a business where the owner has only to keep 10% of inventory on hand all the time and lend out the other 90%?

The idea may sound absurd but this is exactly what banks do all the time. And the FED, through each district bank, lends money every day to those banks that don't meet required reserve ratios, charging interest over night on that loan.

---

1. http://www.govtrack.us/congress/vote.xpd?vote=s1999-35

When I worked at (2) Allied Irish Bank on the cash desk in the early nineties one of our clients was Guinness Peat Aviation (GPA), the largest airline leasing company in the world at the time. A few days before the Christmas holidays, GPA called to announce a massive deposit of cash at the bank: $300 million and wanted a competitive interest rate for over night, actually 3 days due to holiday.

As I was the cash manager that day, I offered the company 5.25% for three days.

They accepted.

So now my job was to call other banks and get a rate from them higher than 5.25%. We would pay GPA the following in interest:

$300,000,000 times 5.25% times 3 (days)/365 = $129,452.05

I had to get a rate higher than that to make money for the bank. I managed to get 5 3/8% or 5 5/16% in some cases, an average of 1/8% over and above the rate we gave GPA.

Thus AIB would receive the following:
$300,000,000 times .125% times 3/365 = $30,821.92

A nice amount of money for making a few calls banks in New York City, three days before Christmas! However, after spending the great part of the morning selling the $300 million and getting a decent spread on it, I was called again by GPA informing me that they'd just received another $200 million, probably from one of their clients an airline company paying for delivery of the jet liners.

2. Author worked as currency options trader in 1994 at AIB in New York City, 405 Park Avenue, and 2nd Floor

Now with just 15 minutes to go to banks closing in London and Europe, 12 noon, I had to frantically make calls to New York based banks and convince them to pay me more than 5 1/4% on $200m.

As sweat began to pour I managed to get $180m at just above the 5 1/4 %, say 5 5/16% making the following for AIB:

$180,000,000 times .0625% times 3/365 = $92,465.75

I still had $20m to get rid of and ended up calling the Bank of Mongolia in New York to put it on deposit with them at 5 9/32% making 1/32 of one percent as follows:

$20,000,000 times .03125% times 3/365 = $5136.98

In other words the extra $200m netted the bank a total of just under $98,000 for a few hours work and effort executed by me!

That was how cash deposits by corporations made money for the bank through interest spreads.

But seventeen years ago complex derivatives were rarities.

The BIS has in one of its reports mentioned the figure $516 trillion as the associated notional value of total outstanding derivatives. The chart (7) below shows how these exotic financial instruments dwarf the combined value of US money supply, US GDP, total value of world stocks and bonds combined. That's 516 versus 165 and if one divides the bigger number by the smaller the picture is quite disturbing indeed.

Chart 7

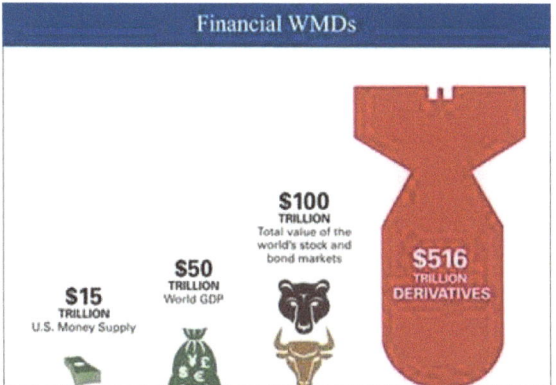

Financial WMD = 516/165 times = 3.12727272727272727 recurring

Source: Market Oracle.co.uk

All of the numbers to the left added equal $165,000,000,000 and if this is divided into the big red bomb number the answer is 3.12727272727272727 into infinity.

So these derivatives so misunderstood by the inventors and traders of them alike are more than three times bigger than the combined totals of the money supply of the US, world GDP and total stocks and bonds.

Most traders don't want to discuss this openly, nor do the leaders in government. But the information is there for all to see in various BIS reports from 2007, 2008 and 2009. Only those expert insiders are truly aware of this financial WMD, but due to mega bonuses earned by Wall Street from these instruments, no body's saying a word.

If one looks at (3) BIS reports over that period one observes the exponential growth in OTC (over the counter) unregulated derivatives.

Many were exotic in nature and complicated in execution. Others became so complicated that the originators of the instruments hardly understood them themselves.

There were: options on currency exchange, interest rate derivatives, CMOs (Collateralized Mortgage Obligations), CDOs (Collateralized Debt Obligations). And other incredibly complicated financial instrument that were originally used for hedging purposes and not for making money by doing nothing.

All of these derivatives operated from sophisticated spreadsheets with cells of formulae based on assumptions about the market, the economy, interest rates etc. Each formula would dictate the values in other cells in the spread sheet and in turn cause an asset to be re-valued almost constantly on a daily basis. When the housing boom was in full bloom several of the big invest banks and financial institutions had one of these cells with complicated formulae at the center of the spread sheet that stupidly assumed house prices would continue to soar over time.

When property prices began to stumble, the tiny formula in the central core of the spread sheet turned out to have a cascading effect on the entire valuation of the asset, rendering it close to worthless. As the house of cards that was the housing market crumbled, so too did the valuation of the stocks in the likes of Lehman Brothers, Bear Stearns, Merrill Lynch, AIG et al.

Then the CEOs and executives of these banks came crying and whined to Hank Paulson (ex-Goldman Sachs) begging for relief.

Paulson attempted to ram down the throats of the tax paying public his version of a bail out: TARP. He was shocked by the reaction of the ordinary Joes.

---

3. *BIS Triennial and semi-annual report on global OTC derivatives – November 2007-BIS.org*

In fact (4) TARP sounded like a financial tarpaulin placed over the mess that was Wall Street at the time. A tarp or tarpaulin is something used to put a cover over or cover-up stuff. The acronym famously granted referred to Troubled Assets Relief Program, a kind of beneficial sounding scheme, or gimmick assisting poor troubled souls in the banking world.

It should have been renamed Totally Astounding Reallocation Program!

Many banks no longer seem fiscally responsible and in fact are teetering on the brink all the time. The FDIC had a watch list of 150 banks at one point that were close to insolvency. Further when TARP has been repaid by all of the recipients of aid, what's stopping the banks from going down the same route again and coming back for more to the FED and Treasury? Why should taxpayers' collected money be re-allocated and engaged in the alleviation of gross financial ineptitude?

From the time of GLBA in 1999 until 2009, the big investment banks had a field day. There were once five, all founded in the eighty-five year period between 1850 (Lehman Brothers) and 1935 (Morgan Stanley); the others, 1869 (Goldman Sachs), 1914 (Merrill Lynch) and 1923 (Bear Stearns).

Now there are two major players, both having converted themselves into commercial banks: Goldman Sachs and Morgan Stanley. The others already commercial banks: JP Morgan Chase and Citibank have both taken TARP and paid it back. From 1999 to 2009 investment banks engaged in reckless financial risk taking, lost billions of dollars, destroyed shareholder value and ate vociferously from the hand of the tax payer via the Treasury. In those ten years the no holds barred de-regulation caused by GLBA incited an investment riot as financial institutions from AIG to Fannie Mae and Freddie Mac stumbled, head first into derivative trading, losing trillions and crying to the FED for help.

---

4. See http://www.sigtarp.gov/reports.shtml - report to Congress July 21st 2009

The FED under Geithner (the $42,702 pseudo-tax dodger) in New York, Greenspan in Washington DC and later Bernanke, flew to the rescue. But that rescue was underwritten by two planks in the financial foundation: 1. Taxpayer compliance; and 2. Treasury issuance of debt through the same banks that were eventually bailed out.

Bear Stearns no longer, sold to JP Morgan Chase for $2 a share; Merrill Lynch swallowed by Bank of America amid serious controversy; and Lehman, allowed to fail with pieces of it sold to a British bank, Barclays.

Monies set aside for bonuses to Goldman Sachs' staff and managing directors in (5) 2009 topped $17 billion. Although the bank received $10 billion in bail outs, it repaid all in full.

5. *http://www.reuters.com/article/idUSTRE5AG5PQ20091119* - *Goldman Sachs makes 272 new managing directors (Reuters, Nov. 19th 2002)*

Chapter 4

McFadden and Butler

Before the enactment of the Federal Reserve Act of 1913 Congress vigorously debated back and forth during the writing and passage of the bill.

Huge changes were to be made preparing the United States economic and monetary system for increased control by a few wealthy families and men, the patriarchs of those families.

One of the most vociferous opponents to these sweeping was one Louis T. McFadden, republican congressman, who had served several years as chairman of the Committee on Banking and Currency. In 1932 he was relegated to member.

During the period 1920 to 1932, McFadden served on this committee and understood from the inside out how the monetary system in general and the FED in particular, actually worked. He saw the United States go through the roaring twenties, the Crash of 1929, its aftermath and the Great Depression.

In 1932 on DATE McFadden made a twenty-five minute speech to Congress on the dangers of the Federal Reserve Bank:

Only two years later retired Major General Smedley D. Butler (USMC) gave testimony to Congress when he detailed a plot into which an attempt was made to have him lead a coup against the FDR administration. According to published articles in the archives of the New York Times, Wall Street Journal and other newspapers at the time, Butler was to lead 500,000 men in a coup against the Washington Roosevelt administration.

In the New York Times report dated November 1934(1), Butler's account of the attempted coup is detailed. It didn't come to pass, but rather than take the United

States from the people through force of arms, the Fed and its supporters took the economic and monetary system by stealth through the destruction of purchasing power of the dollar over time (1a) and the mounding of debt upon the government (and ordinary people) by ensuring the message of indebtedness was spread far and wide throughout the United States of America.

Chart (1a)

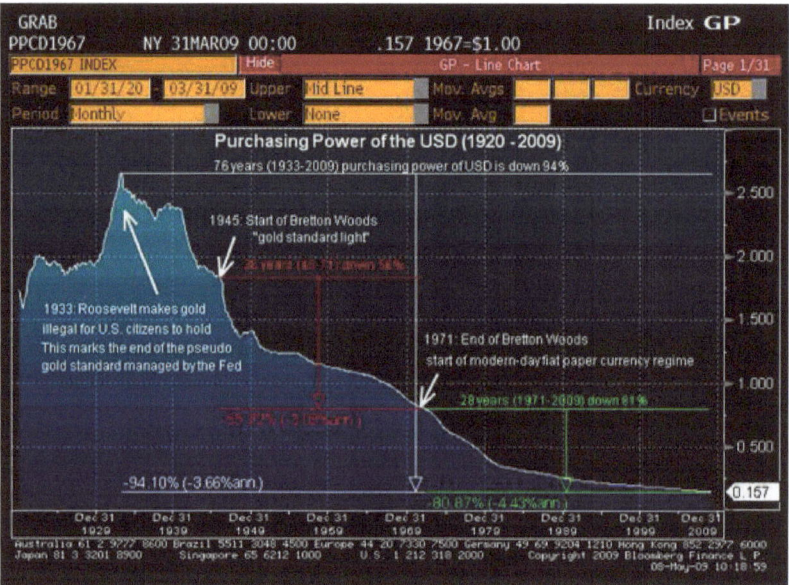

Source: Bloomberg Charts

The chart above shows that in less than seventy years, one generation, the purchasing power (PP) of the USD has actually weakened by a whopping 94%! In plain language, the dollar you had in your pocket in 1929 could buy 94% MORE than the dollar you have in your pocket today. However here's the catch: in 1929 the availability of credit was scarce relative to today. Although many ordinary people owned stocks before the crash, credit cards, loans etc. were not as prolific.

Today, the dollar is worth less, its purchasing power diminished, but the supply of money has expanded dramatically in the form of credit cards, checking accounts, mortgages for houses that many cannot afford. And all the while the money supply increases the banks issue more loans and take in more interest.

The chart below (1c) shows just how fast the money supply grew from 1913 to 2010:

Chart (1c)

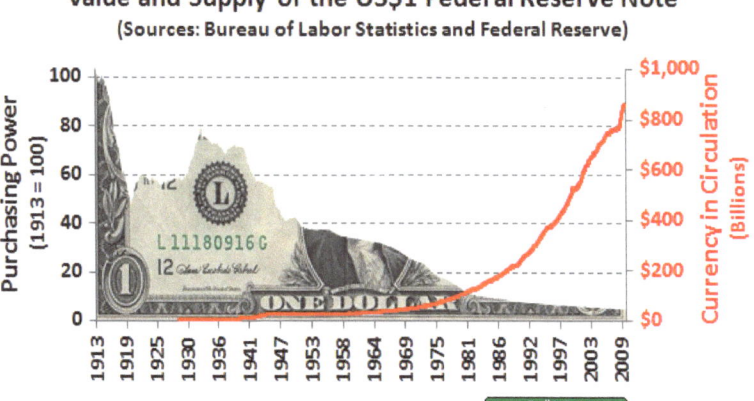

Source: BLS and Federal Reserve

There is an inverse relationship as illustrated in the chart between the PP and the monetary supply. Obviously, basic economics states that when supply is rampant the value of something is degraded. This is the case with the USD. By flooding the economy with credit or money, the people become indebted. And on the exact opposite pole, by limiting the availability of money and/or credit, the people have a miserable time surviving. The chart shows the exact polar opposites in just one generation: 70 years.

Butler was not to be outfoxed by the potential coup planners militarily but unfortunately economically he was.

So he looked at the economic effects of war. Who were the profiteers from war he asked? Who wants war and who fights those wars?

Many years later in his controversial and quiet short, book "War is a Racket", the outspoken Butler wrote (2):

"WAR is a racket. It always has been. It is possibly the oldest, easily the most profitable, surely the most vicious.

Only a small "inside" group knows what it is about. It is conducted for the benefit of the very few, at the expense of the very many. Out of war a few people make huge fortunes.

In the World War [I] a mere handful garnered the profits of the conflict. At least 21,000 new millionaires and billionaires were made in the United States during the World War. That many admitted their huge blood gains in their income tax returns. How many other war millionaires falsified their tax returns, no one knows.

How many of these war millionaires shouldered a rifle? How many of them dug a trench? How many of them knew what it meant to go hungry in a rat-infested dug-out? How many of them spent sleepless, frightened nights, ducking shells and shrapnel and machine gun bullets? How many of them parried a bayonet thrust of an enemy? How many of them were wounded or killed in battle?"

The answer to these questions was a positive zero! None of the ruling elite went to war.

Have times changed in 2010? Look at the number of Senators and Congressmen's offspring that are serving in Iraq or Afghanistan and the numbers are slim.

Butler was no mere leftist talking head spewing out anti-war propaganda or puny armchair theories on war.

He had been a marine for 34 years and was there in the trenches of France, been to China with the Marine Expeditionary Force (1927 – '29), had fought in Central America and Honduras. He had fought with U.S. Marines in the Philippines, had marched on behalf of veterans to Washington after the Great War and vigorously advocated on their behalf.

Butler had witnessed firsthand the real winners in war, the profits from war and to whom that profit went to.

He remarked in his book referring to the Philippines the following:

"We have spent about $600,000,000 in the Philippines in thirty-five years and we (our bankers and industrialists and speculators) have private investments there of less than $200,000,000. At the end of the World War period, as a direct result of our fiddling in international affairs, our national debt had jumped to over $25,000,000,000. Our total favorable trade balance during the twenty-five-year period was about $24,000,000,000."

The Great War ended in 1918 with the U.S. entering one year before the end on April 6th 1917. U.S. national debt after the war was $25,000,000,000. And according to Butler the costs in lives and cash were humongous:

"The World War, rather our brief participation in it, has cost the United States some $52,000,000,000."

So the U.S. government borrowed $25 billion and spent a further $52 billion in one year from 1917 until the end of the war in 1918.

Butler reserved a special attack for the du Pont family, when he referred to the company's profits:

"They were a patriotic corporation. Well, the average earnings of the du Ponts for the period 1910 to 1914 were $6,000,000 a year. It wasn't much, but the du Ponts managed to get along on it."

Along comes the United States' entry and as if by magic:

Now let's look at their average yearly profit during the war years, 1914 to 1918. Fifty-eight million dollars a year profit we find! Nearly ten times that of normal times and the profits of normal times were pretty good, an increase in profits of more than 950 per cent."

Another target of Butler's penmanship was Bethlehem Steel Company, one of the biggest steel manufacturers in the U.S. at the time.

"Take one of our little steel companies that patriotically shunted aside the making of rails and girders and bridges to manufacture war materials. Well, their 1910-1914 yearly earnings averaged $6,000,000: then came the war. And, like loyal citizens, Bethlehem Steel promptly turned to munitions making. Did their profits jump -- or did they let Uncle Sam in for a bargain? Well, their 1914-1918 average was $49,000,000 a year!"

By this time, 1914 to 1918, the Fed had already been in full swing for more than a year and five respectively. As the Treasury was taxing the people, collecting the taxes through the IRS (also founded as a result of the 1913 Federal Income Tax Act, signed into law on February 2nd, 1913), massive amounts were being paid out to du Pont, Bethlehem, US Steel et al. from the taxpayers. And the irony of it all was that those very same tax payers were fighting in German and French trenches.

3. Photo 1. Butler upon retirement at ceremony (circa 1931)

Whether you agree with Butler's assessments on war or not, whether you agree with his comments on the profits from war and it being a racket or not doesn't matter.

What matters is who finances these wars and to who does the profits of war go? Have the nature of wars changed in the hundred years plus since Butler was a marine in the trenches of China in 1900?

Major General Smedley D. Butler died on the summer solstice, 21st June 1940, a full year and half **before** the United States entered World War II on December 8th 1941, one day after the Japanese attack on Pearl Harbor.

Butler's book is no longer in print but can be accessed on the internet for free and is a must read for any aspiring truth seeker.

Shockingly in my lectures to thousands of students during the past few years, few if any had ever heard of Smedley Butler. Even more surprising to me was when I mentioned Butler to a friend of mine, (a major in the U.S. Army who's been to Iraq and Afghanistan) and he responded that he'd never heard of the man! After a brief phone conversation I informed him of the importance of the man. Now he's heard of him and has read widely about him.

Such a man as Butler is a rarity today. In the history books of the United States education system, Butler seems to have been erased from memory.

It is in the battlefield of memory that we learn not to forget history and the intricate connections between economics, politics, war-financing and military conquest. We make a catastrophic mistake in diluting the truth of history since our sons and daughters will remain ignorant and continue making the same insane mistakes of their forefathers.

In the chart on the following page it can be proven that the value of the dollar has been declining steadily over the past fifty three years, (1947 was the first year of CPI data). Beginning in 1947 inflation was measured through the Consumer Price Index (CPI) and since this time the dollar's value has been degraded substantially.

1. *New York Times, November 1934 "*
2. *"War is a Racket" by Smedley D. Butler; published 1935*
3. *Photo 1. Smedley D. Butler upon Retirement*

Source: 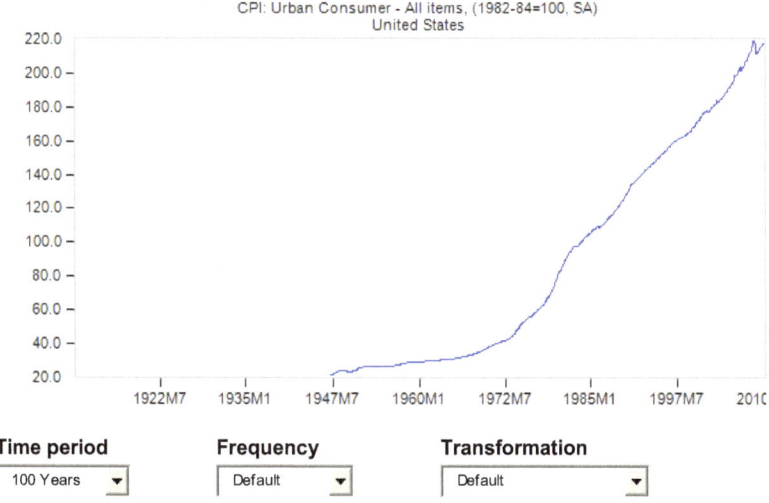 **Moody's** | Economy-com

Chart 2: Inflation since records first began.

What matters in this chart is that when the Fed was formed, money supply was scarce and worth more. But as time went on as shown in the chart above, more money pumped into the economy by the Fed resulted in the value of that money being weakened. Something that might have cost $1 in 1947 would cost seven times more in 1997 or $7 and ten times more in 2007, $10. In other words, ordinary salary and wage earners are earning dollars now that are about ten times **less** valuable than in 1947.

But the key difference is they have access to **more** credit, are indebted through mortgages, credit cards, overdrafts, student loans etc. and are paying interest to banks, the very banks that control and run the Fed.

Chart 2 - from Moody's

Chapter 5

GAO and Treasury

There are two tentacles of government that are inextricably linked: The Government Accountability Office (GAO) and the Treasury.

The GAO is tasked with investigating how the federal government spends taxpayer dollars and is often regarded as the "congressional watchdog".

Well over the past ten years the watchdog has had its work cut out for it given that our national debt stands over $12,000,000,000,000, a mind boggling number.

So the GAO keeps on eye on the money spent while the Treasury through the IRS collects the taxes from the taxpayers, corporations and small to medium sized businesses.

In one of the many reports prepared by the GAO, one makes for quite interesting reading. "Iraq, Pakistan and Afghanistan" was prepared in November, 2009 (1) and details 189 items analyzing the expenditures in these three countries, all monies collected by the Treasury through the IRS via taxes from ordinary people.

One part of the report refers to how the DOD is faring in cost containment in its "war on terror".

In, **"Global War on Terrorism (GWOT):** DOD Needs to More Accurately Capture and Report the Costs of Operation Iraqi Freedom and Operation Enduring Freedom" (2), the GAO reports that the GWOT has cost the DOD $808 billion since 2001. In fact DOD's "reported annual obligations" for the GWOT have increased from just a puny $0.2 billion in fiscal year 2001 to a whopping $162.4 billion in fiscal year 2008.

And despite the myriad of intelligence agencies, counter terrorist data bases, a 23 year old Nigerian can board a plane with a bomb in his underpants!

On Christmas Day, 2009, the crotch bomber boarded a plane and attempted to blow it apart.

He evaded the National Counter Terrorism Center (NCTC), and its parent, Office of the Director of National Intelligence (DNI), CIA, FBI, Homeland Security, NSA, Terrorist Identity Datamart Environment (TIDE) and TSA.

In short he slithered through the bloated national security apparatus.

Yet the GAO cautioned the DOD to reign in its incessant call for further appropriations. And in a mind numbing 29 page report, a 2006 GAO study (3) found that the DOD inventory was so lax that the US Army lost track several airplanes (56), tanks (32) and javelin missile command launch units (36).

In plain language taxpayers money was wasted and military hardware mysteriously was unaccounted for and went missing. The more reading of GAO reports I did, the more I began to realize that the Comptroller General, David Walker must have been the most frustrated man in the United States, as he and his good intentioned staff painstakingly tracked and reported on government spending for thousands or millions of hours, but then to be ignored by the titans of arrogance in the DOD, Rumsfeld et al.

Walker resigned in 2008 and joined the Peter G. Petersen Foundation and is the narrator of the anti-government debt gospel, "I.O.U.S.A.".

1. GAO: Iraq, Afghanistan and Pakistan

2. http://www.gao.gov/docsearch/featured/oif.html GWOT and DOD $808 billion in appropriations

3. GAO-06-1006T

In the documentary, Walker warns the viewer that weapons of mass destruction are of a financial nature and presents a nightmare scenario of wanton government spending, borrowing beyond our means and federal deficits as far as the eye can see.

According to Walker there are four deficits: 1. the federal deficit; 2. the trade deficit; 3. a savings deficit and finally a leadership deficit.

The US government is guilty on all four counts.

Meanwhile the US Treasury is busily formulating reports on this, that and the other. For example Geithner, the Treasury Secretary is responsible for twelve other agencies controlled by the Treasury.

They are: Alcohol, Tobacco Tax and Trade Bureau (ATTB);
Bureau of Engraving and Printing (BEP); Bureau of the Public Debt (BPD); Community Development Financial Institution Fund (CDFI); Financial Crimes and Enforcement Network (FinCen); Financial Management Services (FMS); Inspector General; Treasury Inspector General for Tax Administration (TIGTA); IRS; Office of the Comptroller of the Currency (OCC); Office of Thrift Supervision (OTS); and finally the US Mint, the place where all the pennies, nickels, dimes and quarters are made. Geithner has an exhausting portfolio.

The majority of these agencies are responsible for collecting taxes and distributing those taxes in the form of federal spending. And the taxpayer has absolutely no input into how these monies are distributed.

Debt is also one of the most important mandates of the US Treasury.

In 2008 the Treasury was responsible for the auctioning off $6.7 trillion (4) in securities (government bonds) through 260 public auctions of debt. At time of writing of this book under the upcoming auctions section of the Treasury web site, January 7th, 11th and 14th in 2010 were scheduled dates with 91 day, 182 day , 364 day, 3 year and 10 year bills and notes going on the block.

Who's buying these pieces of paper, backed up by the ever compliant and hard working tax payer?

According to a 2009 GAO study (5) on the Treasury, foreign debt holders had increased their share of total US debt from $1.001 trillion in June 2001 to $3.384 trillion in June 2009.

That's a whopping 338% increase in foreign investors buying up US debt!

And upon maturity guess who foots the bill of the original principal and interest? Answer: my kids, your kids and your grandkids!

Ironically the GAO's motto is "Accountability, Reliability and Integrity", three wonderfully theoretical platitudes. But with $14 trillion and counting in outstanding debt owed by government and 45% of that owned by foreign investors, this trio is quite farcical when applied to the bureaucrats in the US government.

According to CNBC (6) the top 20 holders of the debt include Luxembourg at #15 with $104.2 billion. This is one of the smallest countries in Europe with a population of just 493,500 people. And at number #13 with $119.9 billion is Russia, with president Putin an ex-head of KGB. Caribbean Banking Centers are #10 with $189.7 billion. And oil exporters stand at #9 with $191 billion of the debt. And ironies of ironies our ex-colonial owners, UK, are at #8 with just under one quarter of a trillion or $214 billion. US pension funds at #7 are holders of just under half a trillion or $465.4 billion and #6 are local and state governments, many of whom are supposedly bankrupt or close to bankruptcy, California and New York! The top five are: #5 "Other Investors" with $629.7 billion; #4 is Japan with $711.8 billion, once the largest foreign holder but now eclipsed by China at #3 with $776.4 billion. Number #2, are mutual funds with $769.1.

But by far the most bizarre holder at #1 with a monstrous $4.785 trillion is the Federal Reserve Bank and "intra governmental holdings". The figure was from March 2009 and actually had decreased from an all time high of $4.785 trillion in December 2008 at the height of the financial crisis.

So get this, the Fed which is supposed to monitor the monetary policy of the United States economy, fix over night fed funds rates and generally expand or contract the money supply of the US is the number one owner of federal government debt!

To ordinary tax payers it seems like the printing of dollar bills in Washington is going on incessantly with the entire financial system built upon the energy, dynamism and work of people in various jobs and businesses. And the spending of those dollars collected is being wasted on GWOT in countries far away, bail outs for banks that adopted a casino like addiction to their gambling on the derivatives tables across computer screens in trading floors across the world.

The ever compliant taxpayer has one of two choices: to continue as a mushroom, being in the dark being fed fertilizer or become aware of what exactly is going on and do something about it. Because now is the time. It would be cowardice to wait for another generation to fix this mess.

4. http://www.treasurydirect.gov/indiv/products/prod_auctions_glance.htm
5. GAO-10-88
6. http://www.cnbc.com/id/29880401 "The Biggest Holders of US Government Debt"
7. www.marketoracle.co.uk Outstanding Derivatives Financial WMD

Chapter 6

Death and Taxes

As the old adage goes only two things are certain in life and that's death and taxes.

Taxes are certainly necessary but what most people are sickened about is what those taxes are spent on.

A cursory look at federal spending in 2009 shows that the overwhelming percentage of our taxes collected by the Treasury via the IRS went to pay for three wars, Iraq and Afghanistan and the GWOT.

The two pie charts below (next page) from the US Treasury (1) and Congressional Budget Office (2), (CBO) illustrate the appetites of Treasury, interest servicing of the debt, the DOD and the Pentagon.

US Army personnel I know personally were sent into battle in Iraq with shoddy equipment Humvees with no steel enforcement, fatigues for the jungle not the desert.

Where is all this money spent on defense going?

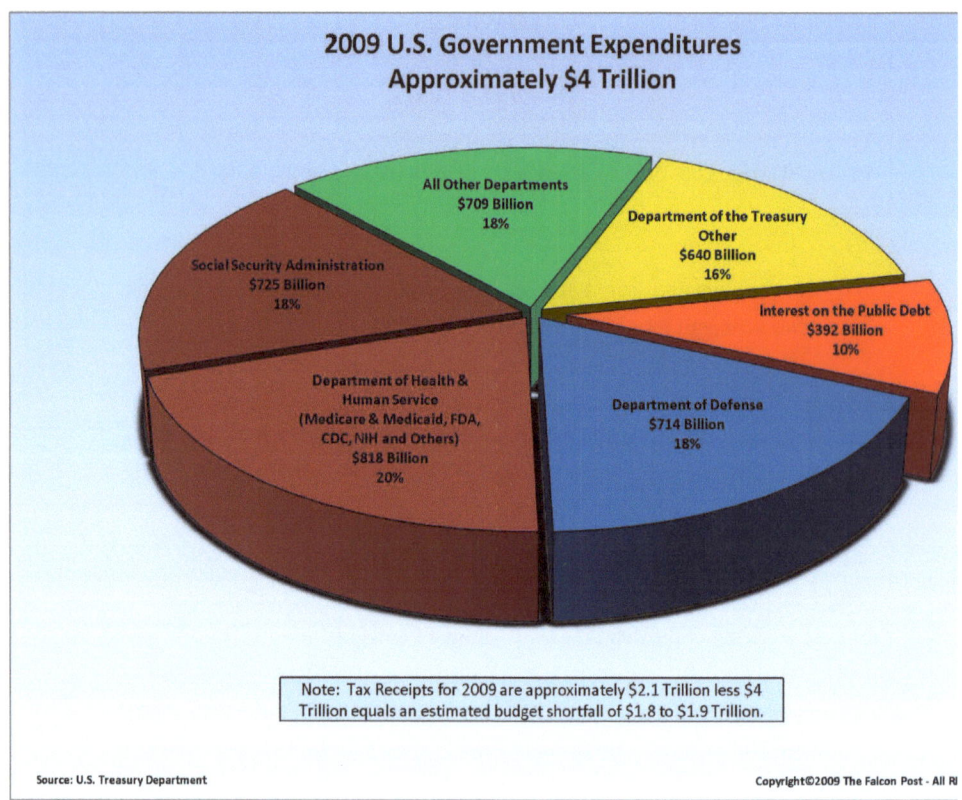

1. Chart 1. 2009 U.S. Government Spending

What I find disturbing about this chart is the "Department of the Treasury – Other" accounts for $640 billion or 16% of 2009 expenditures. Also DOD, interest and Treasury combined accounts for a whopping $1.746 trillion dollars in expenditures.

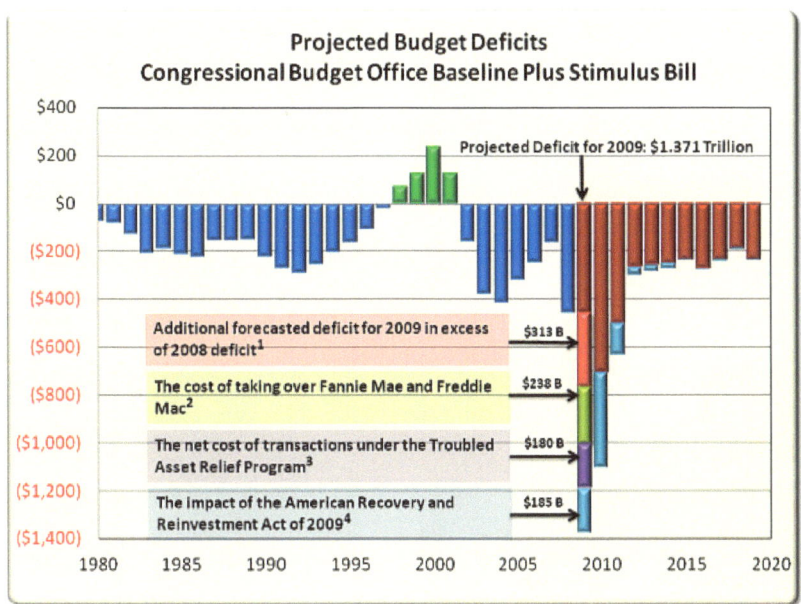

Source: The Budget and Economic Outlook: Years 2009 to 2019 and Letter dated February 13, 2009 from CBO to Speaker Pelosi

2. Chart 2. CBO Projections: 2009 and Beyond.

In his land mark book published in 1971, "The Pentagon Propaganda Machine", Senator J. William Fulbright writes that, "Violence is our most important product." Since the early 1950s the US has been "spending nearly $80 billion a year on the military".

That was written back in the 1970s. Now in the 2010's we're spending in the hundreds of billions!

1. US Treasury Department, Government Spending
2. Congressional Budget Office 2009 Projections

According the graph above, the only time the federal government had a budget surplus, was in the period 1996 to about 1999. 1998 showed a surplus of almost $250 billion.

The government that fiscal year took in one quarter of a trillion more than it spent according to published CBO reports.

Shockingly since the late nineties and into the 2000s surpluses have gone the way of dinosaurs and are predicted to never again appear on government spending charts and graphs.

There are two main ways the government can close these gaps: borrow more or raise taxes and cut services. No politician wants to swallow the hard medicine on raising taxes across the board. So like a heroin addict needing a fix, borrowing is the financial and politically expedient fix.

As the United States ramps up its GWOT and sends another 30,000 troops to the mountains of Afghanistan since Fulbright's era, we have become the world leader in borrowing and sales of defense equipment.

Districts where the missiles, tanks and bombs are manufactured are represented by various senators and congressmen. When jobs that need DOD funding in these munitions are at risk, no politician, regardless of party affiliation is going to vote against any defense appropriations bill.

An example: the missing javelin missile command launch units. In the eyes of the military, this weapon is number one and loved by its users.

Where is this super-weapon manufactured? Answer: In several states across the United States.

Who makes it? Answer: Raytheon. Raytheon's web site shows the exact locations where these and many other weapons systems are manufactured.

Neither senator nor congressman will vote against defense appropriations in his or her district, since defense jobs will be lost as a result.

Such voting would be political suicide.

The top defense contractors are shown in table below (3):

Contractor	2006 Defense Revenue (mil)	2000 Defense Revenue (mil)	% Change	2006 Profit (mil)	2000 Profit (mil)	% Change
Lockheed Martin	$36,090	$18,000	101%	$1,825	$382	378%
Boeing	$30,800	$17,000	81%	$2,572	$2,309	11%
Northrop Grumman	$23,649	$5,600	322%	$1,400	$467	200%
Raytheon	$19,500	$14,033	39%	$871	$404	116%
General Dynamics	$18,769	$6,542	187%	$1,461	$880	66%
Totals	$128,808	$61,175	111%	$8,129	$4,442	83%

Source: DefenseNews

3. Table 1 – Top 5 Defense Contractors from 2006

With revenue up for Raytheon from $14 billion to $19.5 billion is just six years, clearly the GWOT has been a Godsend to this defense contractor. But the real winner here since 2000 is Northrop Grumman with an increase of 322% in revenue in just six years.

And for fiscal 2010 these top five are projected to make even more from the GWOT, all funded by the taxes collected by the Treasury via the IRS. Meanwhile, the infrastructure of many states in this country is crumbling.

3: Table 1. Shows top Defense Contractors in 2006; Defense News

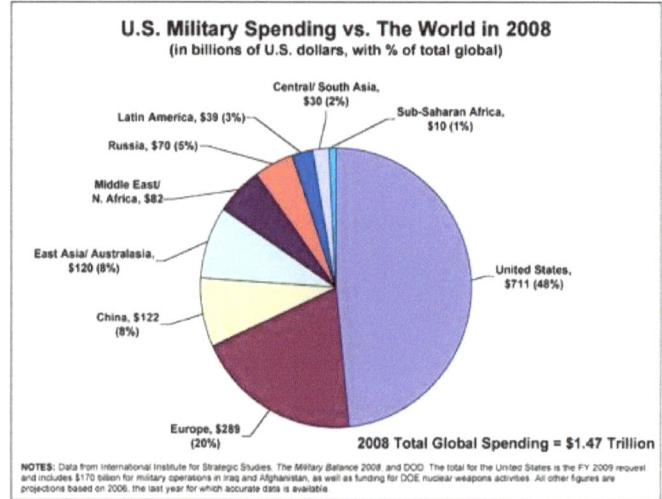

4. Chart 3. Global Military Spending; Institute of Strategic Studies

And according to the Institute of Strategic Studies, the United States spends more military hardware than the countries China, Russia and the entire continent of Europe combined (4).

The United States accounts for 48% of global military spending having spent $711 billion in 2008 out of the total globally of $1.47 trillion.

Global defense spending is predicted to grow into the $2-3 trillions over the next decade with the US leading the world in defense spending.

Country	Military Spending (Billions of $)
United States	$711.0
China	$121.9
Russia	$70.0
United Kingdom	$55.4
France	$54.0
Japan	$41.1
Germany	$37.8
Italy	$30.6
Saudi Arabia	$29.5
South Korea	$24.6
India	$22.4
Australia	$17.2

Sources: International Institute for Strategic Studies

5. Table 2: Top Spender of Top 12 Countries (2008)

The United States has a population of about 303.8 million (est. 2008) people and accounts for about 5% of the world's population (5). But yet it accounts for 45% of expenditures on military equipment, mostly destined for other countries and used against the citizens of those countries to repress them.

And the US taxpayer has his or her pockets rifled every April 15th when tax return time comes and the IRS rakes in trillions, hand it over to the Treasury who in turn gives a bulging bag of money in appropriations to the DOD.

What states in the US provide for the most defense contracting jobs? In Missouri in 2006 according to a Missouri Economic Research and Information Center (MERIC) 2008 report, "Missouri Impact Brief: US DOD Contract Spending", $13.5 billion in defense contracts was awarded to Missouri vendors in 2006 (7).

And on page three of the same report surrounding states including: Illinois, Tennessee, Kentucky, Arkansas, Oklahoma, Kansas, Nebraska and Iowa (collectively the Mid-West) had vendors awarded in excess of $13 billion in defense contracts (8).

These nine states combined accounted for $25 billion in awards by DOD. Each award equals jobs for each state.

Allied to all the jobs created by the DOD in awarding these contracts Missouri is home to two important armed services bases: Fort Leonard Wood (US Army) and Whiteman Air Force Base (USAF), both of which employ tens of thousands of military personnel.

According to the economic impact brief, over 14,000 at Fort Leonard Wood with a payroll of $611 million, while Whiteman Air Force Base employed over 4,000 with a payroll of $190 million (9).

This is data on jobs and payroll and awards to just one state with a population of 5.6 million and an unemployment rate of 9.5% (10) (November 2009), according to MERIC.

Why would local politicians and those representing the state in Washington DC vote against any defense appropriations bills with so many jobs at stake in the defense industry? On December 19th 2009, on a Saturday, a vote in the Senate on defense appropriations, had 88-10 votes cast to allow congress spend $636 billion on the Pentagon in fiscal 2010.

The ten who voted against the bill included one Democrat and nine Republicans. According to the US Senate roll call, during the vote to pass HR-3326, in vote #384 of the 88 yeas Alexander Republican (R), TN was one. So too was Begich a Democrat (D), AK. Another yea was Durban (D), IL and McCaskill (D), Bond (R) both of Missouri (MO).

Fiscal responsibility is not a partisan issue. But going by the recent congressional votes on appropriations for a myriad of projects, there seems to be absolutely no restraint. In fact quite the opposite since the Senate and Congress look at funding as a spigot that they can open at will – that being the Treasury and the IRS tax collection system both of which act as a faucet of money.

Why would these senators from the cluster of mid-west states mentioned in the economic impact brief vote against increased Pentagon appropriations?

They would not, because if they did the voters who are employed by the defense contractors and work at the various forts and bases would surely vote them out on their back side!

4. *Chart 3. www.IISS.org Global Military Spending*

5. *Table 2. Top 12 Spenders www.IISS.org*

6. *C.I.A. World Fact Book*

7. *www.missourieconomy.org/pdfs/dod_spending_jan08*

8. *Page 3; Ibid. See Map.*

9. *Ibid*

10. *MERIC www.missourieconomy.org*

11. *The Hill http://thehill.com/homenews/senate/73049-defense-appropriations-bill-passes-senate-88-10-clearing-way-for-health-bill*

12. *HR-3326*

http://www.senate.gov/legislative/LIS/roll_call_lists/vote_menu_111_1.htm

Chapter 7

Big Brother and the Long War – 50 Years and Beyond

Freedom of Information Act requests (FOIA) have unearthed documents written by the Pentagon outlining the long term war against fundamentalist Islam. This arc of war begins in the Middle East and comes across Europe to the United States.

In a post-911 world there is a need for the DOD and the Pentagon to justify massive spending and with the collapse of the Berlin Wall and the last vestiges of Communism, GWOT filled that void.

When I worked as a journalist for BSN (1) in New York City I covered terrorist financing, identity theft, cyber security and money laundering, all very interesting areas to report on. Under the Treasury, the Office of Foreign Assets Control (OFAC) had authority to list known terrorists who were prevented from opening bank accounts anywhere in the United States.

This OFAC list as it became known is prepared almost daily and updated on the OFAC website, detailing the names and passport numbers of Specially Designated Nationals (SGNs) (2). When I wrote for BSN in 2003, I began to see a proliferation of "Cyber Security Consultant" businesses, mostly with expertise in bank security and computer security. Many had special "vulnerability" expertise pertaining to networks. In the intervening years from 2003 to 2010, many of these companies went by the wayside, while others went on to become multi-billion dollar enterprises.

1. *Bank Security News; August 20th, 2003 PDF File in Author's possession*

The point here is that 911 spawned a huge industry in the War on Terror (WOT). And the GWOT as it became known. In tandem another long drawn out war was to be initiated and named Global Struggle against Violent Extremism with the acronym G-SAVE.

Most of this violent extremism emanated out of the Middle East from countries that were either getting massive funding in "military aid" from the United States or recent countries added to the Obama list of citizens finding it increasingly difficult to travel to the U.S.: Afghanistan, Algeria, Cuba, Iran, Iraq, Lebanon, Libya, Nigeria, Pakistan, Saudi Arabia, Somalia, Sudan, Syria, and Yemen. Anyone attempting to board a plane and enter the United States from one of these fourteen countries will have problems.

On February 3rd 2006 the Pentagon unveiled their 20 year plan and according to the Washington Post (2a):

"the military and the Bush administration are now calling the "long war," likened al Qaeda leader Osama bin Laden to Adolf Hitler and Vladimir Lenin while urging Americans not to give in on the battle of wills that could stretch for years."

In addition the story mentions a time span, twenty years and beyond. This was the initiation of the GWOT that has been continued under the Obama administration and funded as usual by the compliant taxpayer.

2. OFAC List January 1, 2010
http://www.treas.gov/offices/enforcement/ofac/sdn/t11sdnew.pdf

2a. Washington Post; 2/3/2006 Pentagon Unveils Plan

The paper added that:

"The speech, which aides said was titled "The Long War," came on the eve of the Pentagon's release of its Quadrennial Defense Review (QDR), which sets out plans for how the U.S. military will address major security challenges 20 years into the future.... The QDR strategy draws heavily on lessons learned by the military from the wars in Iraq and Afghanistan and the worldwide campaign against terrorism, shifting the Pentagon's emphasis away from conventional warfare of the Cold War era toward three new areas."

With the end of the Cold War other avenues in defense had to be tread and they were broken into three areas according to Donald Rumsfeld who set off on the first path when he stated that:

"First are "irregular" conflicts against insurgents, terrorists and other non-state enemies. Iraq and Afghanistan are the "early battles" in the campaign against Islamic extremists and terrorists, who are "profoundly more dangerous" than in the past because of technological advances that allow them to operate globally, said Deputy Defense Secretary Gordon R. England in an address on Wednesday.

The QDR also focuses on defending the U.S. homeland against "catastrophic" attacks such as with nuclear, chemical or biological weapons. Finally, it sets out plans for deterring the rising military heft of major powers such as China."

At the time of writing of this book (early 2010), the Obama administration was mulling over the deployment of troops to Yemen where an apparent new terrorist outfit were operating.

In an excellent story in the Asia Times (4), ex-Ambassador M.K. Bhadramkumar writing on January 8th and 9th reported that for the U.S. to gain a better foothold in the region it was necessary to control key sea lanes:

"Control of Aden and the Malacca Strait will put the US in an unassailable position in the "great game" of the Indian Ocean. The sea lanes of the Indian

Ocean are literally the jugular veins of China's economy. By controlling them, Washington sends a strong message to Beijing that any notions by the latter that the US is a declining power in Asia would be nothing more than an extravagant indulgence in fantasy....You cannot fight China without occupying Yemen."

And ever since the underpants bomber's attempt to blow up an airliner, a new organization seems to have emerged, al Qaeda in the Arabian Peninsula, or AQAP.

This new terrorist entity AQAP is conveniently based in Yemen, the exact country that has a most important coastal geography where oil routes are concerned.

So as the Pentagon defines new enemies externally, the internal protection of U.S. citizens, demands increased funding as well.

In 2009 the Department of Homeland Security (DHS) (3) asked for $50.5 billion in funding, an increase of 6.8% over 2008 fiscal year. A year later, Obama's new point person on protecting the homeland, Janet Napolitano asked in May 2009 for $55.1 billion for fiscal year 2010, an almost 10% increase from 2009. As an ex-governor of Arizona who oversaw a huge increase in illegal immigration into Arizona (and accompanying crime), Napolitano didn't do a great job in protecting Arizonans. An increase in violence amongst the Mexican cartels inside Arizona, defined much of her tenure. In a lengthy piece in the Village Voice (5), Michael Lacey paints a no holes barred picture of Napolitano's failure to deal with "security" or insecurity! In 2010, she's looking for over $50 billion for protection of the entire country! Guess who's funding this ineptitude? Yes spot on, the tax payer who has to be harassed every time he or she takes a plane to travel inside or outside of the country.

But we are assured that DHS will have the necessary machines in place to "detect" explosive devices. Ex-DHS czar Chertoff is now using his illustrious contacts to flog us these machines with his new company, the Chertoff Group. These machines cost millions more than a simple canine substitute, but Chertoff won't profit from dogs.

According to Mother Jones (6) body scanners are the way to go these days.

Rapiscan Systems and Chertoff will have us all in line for hours at a time and taxes will fund the entire escapade: "The body scanner is sure to get a go-ahead because of the illustrious personages hawking them. Chief among them is former DHS secretary Michael Chertoff, who now heads the Chertoff Group, which represents one of the leading manufacturers of whole-body-imaging machines, Rapiscan Systems. For days after the attack, Chertoff made the rounds on the media promoting the scanners, calling the bombing attempt "a very vivid lesson in the value of that machinery"—all without disclosing his relationship to Rapiscan."

3. DHS Fact Sheet; 2009 and 2010
http://www.dhs.gov/xnews/releases/pr_1202151112290.shtm
http://www.dhs.gov/ynews/releases/pr_124171525272 9.shtm
3a. "Russia, China, Iran Redraw Energy Map", by MK Bhadrakumar; Asia Times
http://www.atimes.com/atimes/Central_Asia/LA08Ag01.html
4. Ibid: "Obama's Yemeni Odyssey Targets China"
http://www.atimes.com/atimes/Middle_East/LA09Ak02.html
5. "Janet Napolitano = Homeland Futility" by Michael Lacey http://www.villagevoice.com/2008-11-26/news/janet-napolitano-homeland-futility-mexico-border/

When I worked covering this emerging market of security and terror combat through cyber security and airport security methods, I never envisaged such an exponential growth in ex-government big wigs setting up "consultant groups" and "experts" in this and that "vulnerability"

The list of ex-heads of various government departments going into the "protection of the homeland" is long and the compliance of the tax payer to continue funding these gimmicks is disturbing. On the inside taxpayers are funding DHS and other homeland related schemes (Border Patrol, F.B.I. etc.), while on the outside, DHS is funding its monstrosities of budgets for a myriad of DHS controlled sub-departments.

A quick FOIA request form on the DHS website (7) reveals just how many different departments that DHS is actually responsible for. (Chart (1) below)

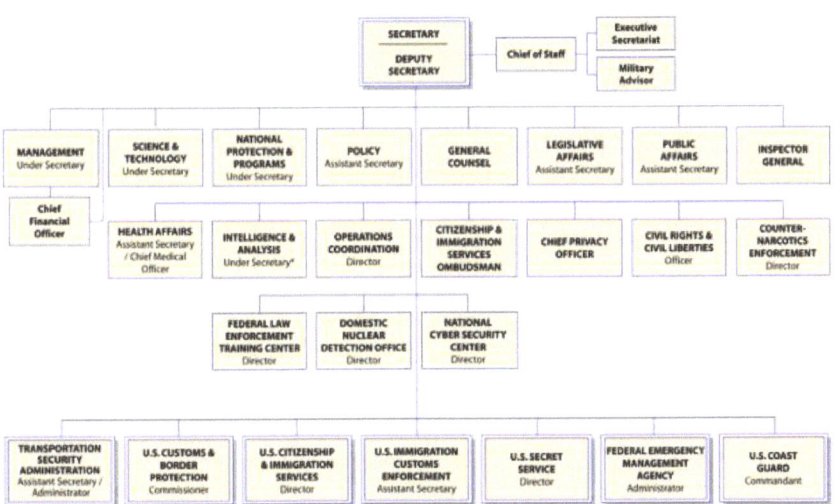

6. "The Airport Scanner Scam" by James Ridgeway

http://motherjones.com/mojo/2010/01/airport-scanner-scam

7. http://www.dhs.gov/xlibrary/assets/FOIA_FedReg_Notice.pdf

Chart 1: Source DHS.gov

And for DOD, with *33 sub-departments* in all, each with its own distinct FOIA procedure requirement a labyrinthine bureaucracy is funded by the taxpayer.

Is it any wonder that the DOD when audited by the GAO was unable to account for $1,000,000,000,000? Here's what $1,000,000,000,000 looks like.

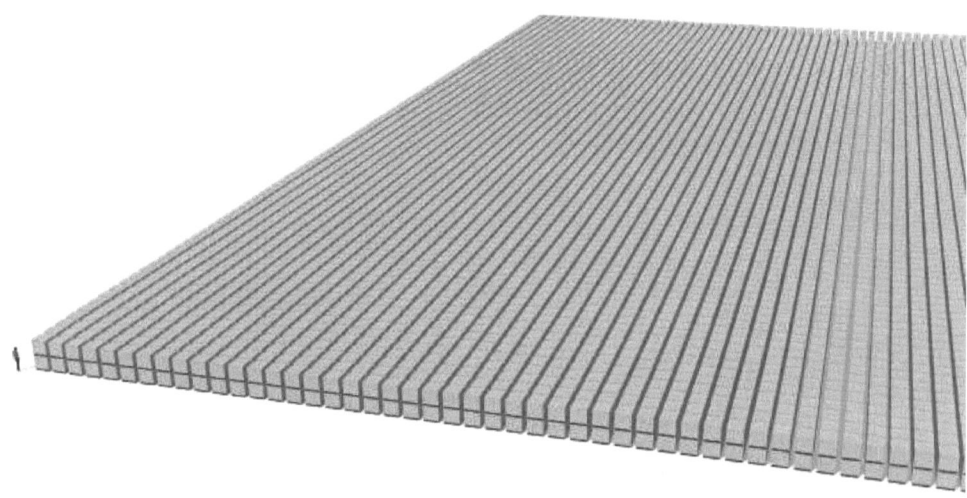

With 33 bureaucracies (7a) responsible for every single FOIA request it boggles the mind how these entities could ever pass along pertinent intelligence to one another to prevent a catastrophic attack on the U.S.

Ex-C.I.A. agent Robert Baer in his excellent book "See No Evil" (8) (later the basis of the movie, "Syriana") lamented the lack of human intelligence (Hum-Int) in his latter years at the agency, complaining that armchair analysts with little or no field work were climbing head over backwards into top positions at the agency.

A farcical situation built on politics.

In the preface to his book Baer states that:

"Like the rest of Washington, the C.I.A. had fallen in love with technology. The theory was that satellites, the Internet, electronic intercepts, even academic publications would tell us what we needed to know.... Running our own agents had become too messy. In 1995 the agency handed the title of director of operations to an analyst who had never served overseas"

The Director of Operations Baer refers to in this passage was Nora Slatkin (9) appointed by John Deutch then Director of Central Intelligence (DCI).

Fifteen years later both Slatkin and Deutch have moved on from the agency.

John Deutch works at MIT as a professor. In a controversial end to his career he was investigated by CIA for security breaches. Clinton pardoned Deutch on his last day in office. Professor Deutch teaches at the chemistry department in MIT.

Slatkin now works for Citigroup, (a TARP recipient of $25 billion in tax payers' hard earned money) as senior manager for government relations.

With no field experience in the CIA, according to her resume posted on LinkedIn, Slatkin worked at the CBO from 1979 to 1985 as a defense analyst. While Robert Baer, a fluent Arabic speaker was risking his life in the Middle East, Slatkin was working at a desk job at the CBO. After her two year stint at CIA (1995 to 1997) she landed a plum job at Citigroup where she's been for almost twelve years.

These are just some of the ex-government officials moving from public to private sector jobs when the circumstances suit.

The next chapter will focus on how tax payers' money is being spent on another huge gobbler of federal spending, Department of Health and Human Services, administrators of Medicaid and Medicare.

Allied to this I will discuss the Social Security Administration.

Both of these combined soaked up $818 billion (20%) and $725 billion (18%) respectively of total spending. In 2009 38% or $1.543 trillion of taxpayers' money was shoveled into the health of the underclass and the retirement of older workers.

7a. FOIA websites "Other Federal Agencies" http://www.justice.gov/oip/other_age.htm

8. From Preface of: "See No Evil – The True Story of a Ground Soldier in the CIA's War against Terrorism", by Robert Baer (2003)

9. "DCI Announces Senior Personnel Appointments" CIA Press Office https://www.cia.gov/news-information/press-releases-statements/press-release-archive-1995/pr51795.html

10. Nora Slatkin – LinkedIn Profile (updated 2010)
http://www.linkedin.com/pub/nora-slatkin/6/2a8/44a

Chapter 8

Healthy, Retired or Hospitalized

Universal healthcare is a wonderful campaign slogan.

But as 2011 eases along toward 2012 and election season again, the promises of candidate Obama and president Obama, have taken a huge turn.

The healthcare debate has bombarded and bamboozled our minds from television and newspaper coverage to internet blogs and town hall meetings.

The bill itself is over 2,000 pages long and can be accessed by going to H.R. 3200 on the government website (1). How the administration intends to pay for this well intentioned bill is not clear. I'd bet through borrowing and having the tax payer repay the maturing bonds, with requested principal and promised interest.

When social security was set up in the mid-1930s there were three workers to every retiree and this went on into the forties and fifties.

It wasn't until the 1960s that this ratio of 3:1 began to change.

Those baby boomers born after World War II when veterans returned, settled down and began to procreate were in their early twenties in the 1960s.

In the years 1960 to 1970, there were about 2:1 workers employed to those retiring and as the 1980s and 1990s arrived the ratio had shrunk to about 1:1 and is continuing to shrink. By the early 2000s it had begun to reverse. There were more people retiring than were working and allied to this the Baby boomers who in early 2000s were in their early, mid or late sixties, a demographic nightmare was about to unfold. (See Chart next page)

1. *http://www.healthreform.gov/*

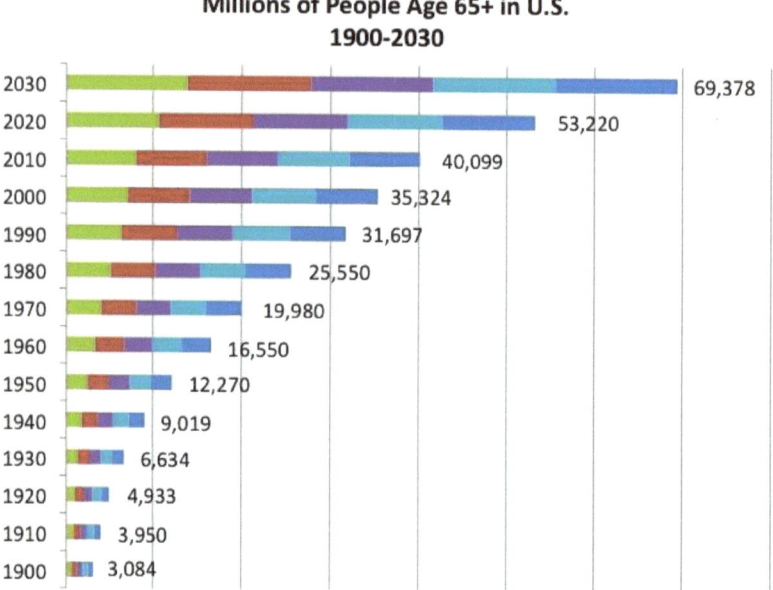

Chart 1: Census Data (Projected from 2010 to 2030)

Over the next few years the number of workers to retirees will reverse and instead of 1:1, the reality of the ratio will look more like 1:2 with TWICE the number of retirees to workers.

The mathematics of the social security system will not add up.

But projected social security payments and Medicare payments are based on the population of workers versus retirees of 3:1 or 2:1, a nightmare of demographic proportions.

As workers age and retire, so too do they get sick.

The chart above predicts a 69.3 million population of sixty-five and older many with health issues.

Who will care for them? What will Medicare look like in 2030? How will it be funded at current rates?

These questions are just the tip of the demographic ice berg and the twin Titanic of Medicare and Social Security are sailing at full speed into that ice berg.

Finally G.W. Bush enacted Medicare Part D (1), which will cost the taxpayer a whopping 5% of total US GDP by 2030 (see chart below). That is the equivalent of about $750 billion (5% of 2011 US GDP) or ¾ of one trillion dollars!

Medicare's Shortfall Due to Increased Expenditures

Medicare's projected funding shortfall is due to increases in expenditures, not decreases in income. Projected income for Medicare Part A as a percentage of GDP will drop only slightly, and it will increase for Medicare Parts B and D. In both cases, expenditures are projected to drastically outpace income.

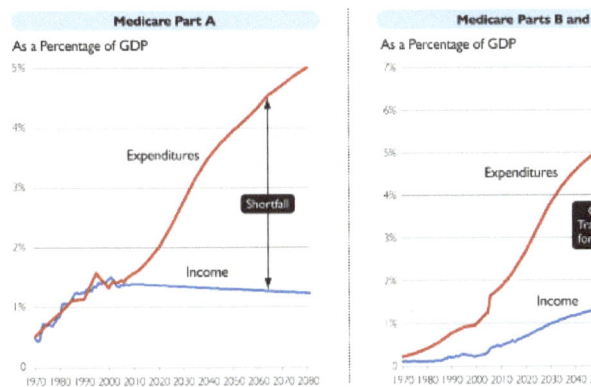

Chart 2: Source: Heritage.Org (2009)

1. http://www.medicare.gov/navigation/medicare-basics/medicare-benefits/part-d.aspx

Chapter 9

A Creature Created on an Island

For many, the creation of the Fed was a shadowy decision taken during the last days of 1910, a full three years before the 1913 law was enacted establishing the bank.

On November 22nd 1910, a group of leading East coast, powerful financiers took a train from a Hoboken train station in New Jersey to an undisclosed location. Aboard that train were Frank Vanderlip, president of National City Bank, New York (later became Citibank), Henry P. Davison, senior partner, J.P. Morgan Company (later become JP Morgan Chase) and Charles D. Norton, president of the Morgan-dominated First National Bank of New York and Paul Warburg of Kuhn, Loeb another not so known but up and coming bank.

This cabal was destined to lay the foundation for the Federal Reserve Bank (FRB) that would come into being in late 1913.

The undisclosed location was Jekyll Island. Where is this strange sounding place?

Jekyll Island is about midway between Jacksonville, Florida and Savannah, Georgia, off the coast of Georgia. The island itself looks like a Southern version of Manhattan Island in New York City.

One hundred years later it has its own website with the slogan: "It's All Good" (1). But in late 1910 it was a secret getaway for the super-rich to design a monetary architecture for the burgeoning United States economy.

Three names are intimately connected to reports relating to Jekyll Island and the origins of the Fed. The first Eustace Mullins, born 1923 and author of the 1952 book, "Secrets of the Federal Reserve; the second: G. Edward Griffin, born 1931 and author of, "The Creature from Jekyll Island" (first printed 1994) and William Greider, author of the seminal book "Secrets of the Temple: How the Federal Reserve Runs the Country" (1987) (2).

Back to Jekyll Island: In 1886 the entire place was purchased by a group of millionaires and converted into a club for the super-rich, a place where they could all get together and discuss the important issues of the time. Within 14 years almost 1/6 of the world's wealth was represented by the club's roster. Names of famous families with fortunes travelled there unhindered by the unclean masses. People like Astor, Vanderbilt, Morgan and Pulitzer were members of the low-key and secluded club on the 17.3 square mile island off the coast of Georgia. Rules of the club stipulated that a limit of 100 members be imposed to maintain exclusivity.

Much speculation has been made about what was discussed and decided at the meeting in November 1910. What's important to point out is the caliber of men in attendance and the economic environment at the time.

Fed and Treasury Duets

The table below (Table 1) shows the list of Treasury Secretaries and Fed Chairmen, with longest serving nineteen years and the shortest, less than one year. Curiously Alan Greenspan accepted a knighthood from Queen Elizabeth II in 2002, an act not in keeping with the United States Constitution (1). Greenspan is now "Knight Commander of the British Empire" (KBE).

Just whose interests did Greenspan stand for exactly? The British Royal Family? The banking elite? What exactly was "global stability"? Could it have been the preparation of a global architecture for a more cohesive monetary system of control?

1. *www.jekyllisland.com*

Federal Reserve Chairmen and Treasury Secretaries 1913-2011

Fed Chairmen	Years in Office	Overlapping Treasury Secretaries
Charles Hamlin	1914-1916	William G. McAdoo 1913-18
W.P.G Harding	1916-1922*	Carter Glass 1918-20
Daniel R. Crissinger	1923-1927	Andrew Mellon 1921-32
Roy A. Young	1927-1930**	Andrew Mellon
Eugene Meyer	1930-1933***	Ogden Mills 1932-33
		William Woodin 1933
Marriner S. Eccles	1934-1948^	Henry Morgenthau 1934-45
		Fred Vinson 1945-46
Thomas B. McCabe	1948-1951	John Snyder 1946-53
Wm. McC. Martin, Jnr	1951-1970	George Humphrey 1953-57
		Robert Anderson 1953-61
		Douglas Dillon 1961-65
		Henry Fowler 1965-68
		Joseph Barr 1968-69
Arthur F. Burns	1970-1978	David Kennedy 1969-71
		John Connally 1971-72
		George Schultz 1972-74
		William Simon 1974-77
G. William Miller	1978-1979	Michael Blumenthal 1977-79
Paul A. Volcker	1979-1987	William Miller 1979-81
		Donald Reagan 1981-85
		James Baker 1985-88
Alan Greenspan	1987-2006^^	Nicholas Brady 1988-93
		Lloyd Bentsen 1993-94
		Robert Rubin 1995-99
		Lawrence Summers 1999-01

		Paul O'Neill 2001-02
		John Snow 2003-06
		Henry Paulson 2006-09
Ben S. Bernanke	2006-	Timothy Geithner 2009

Table 1 Collated by author January 14, 2010

Geithner was president of the Federal Reserve Bank of New York from 2003 to 2009 where he oversaw (or turned a blind eye to) the implosion of Bear Stearns and Lehman Brothers and facilitated the bailout of AIG with taxpayers' money. AIG of which much has been written was the biggest underwriter of insurance of Credit Default Swaps (CDS) and in 2008 had contracts insuring billions of these "securities" and was given $182 billion in bail outs (3)

1. Article 1, Section 9 of the U.S. Constitution states that:
"No title of nobility shall be granted to by the United States; And no Person holding any Office of Profit or Trust under them, shall, without the Consent of the Congress, accept of any present, Emolument, Office, or Title, of any kind whatever, from any King, Prince or foreign State."

2. When the author of the present book attempted to take these books out on loan from the college library, he was informed that none of the three were held at the library, quite curious given that the history of U.S. monetary policy was contained in all three.

3. "Tim Geithner's Very Bad Week", by Michael Corkery;
http://blogs.wsj.com/deals/2010/01/08/tim-geithners-very-bad-week/
SIGTARP.gov pdf

Table 1 Fed and Treasury, chairmen and secretaries 1914-2010.
    Historical Notes- *Served during WW I; **Served during the Crash of 1929;
    *** Served during the Great Depression; ^Served during WW II;
    ^^Served during the massive expansion of credit, housing and stock booms and was knighted by the British
    in 2002 for "contribution to global stability"
    http://archives.cnn.com/2002/WORLD/europe/09/26/greenspan.knighthood/

Chapter 10

Flatten the Damn Taxes

A flat tax versus a fat tax: that is the question.

The roots of the IRS go back to 1862 and then to 1913 when the 16th amendment to the U.S. Constitution giving Congress the power to enact the Income Tax Act.

As April 15th approaches every year tension, anxiety and anger set in across the United States. It represents the deadline to file a tax return with the IRS, the collection apparatus for the Treasury. In 2010 the IRS employed 106,000 people in four primary divisions and another eight principal offices (see IRS.gov for "Organizational Chart"). According to several studies conducted by a variety of foundations (1) and institutes, there are currently 893 different forms printed by the IRS pertaining to tax returns. Flat tax advocates would cut this number to just two: one for labor income, the other for business and capital income.

If the flat tax on labor income was 10%, a household earning joint income of $50,000 would pay $5000 in income tax. No long forms to be filled in. No long lines at the post office on April 15th. Given that U.S. median income is $50,233 according to reliable estimates, with 155 million people holding down a job, this flat tax would yield: $5000 x 155,000,000=$775,000,000,000 tax revenue from labor. And further every worker/taxpayer would keep $45,000 of their own income versus only $32,000 currently.

Even Herman Cain the Republican nominee has a so-called "9-9-9" plan: 9% income tax, 9% business tax, 9% national sales tax 9%.

This all sounds so simple. Why hasn't it been implemented?

The reason: entrenched interests in the accounting, legal, and taxation industries make billions from decoding the extremely complex and labyrinthine tax code and a simpler code would terminate these career tax preparers.

Open secrets.org (2), an excellent site that tracks lobbyists and campaign contributors shows the top heavy hitters and how much they spent on lobbying. At #38 is the accounting firm Ernst and Young that contributed over $17 million over 1989 to 2009 to both parties. Another firm in the accounting game, Deloitte Touche Tohmatsu gave $15.9 million over the same period, followed by Price Waterhouse Coopers, #49 who gave $15.3 million.

Regardless of who was in power during the period, accounting firms gave to maintain the status quo and the consequential tax complexities from which they earned substantial profits. The overall accounting industry gave a whopping $117 million from 1990 to 2010 to both parties. This number included PACs, individual firms and soft money.

Lawyers and Law firms, many representing companies with a substantial taxation business gave over $1 billion to both parties 73% to democrats and 26% to republicans. In the 2008 election cycle lawyers and law firms handed over $233 million in lobbying fees, the most ever with 76% going to democrats. Already for the 2010 election cycle $43 million has been handed over.

Why would Congress enact a flat tax law with so much money sloshing about the place?

Between 1998 and 2009 total lobbyist spending increased from $1.44 billion to $2.51 billion. The number of lobbyists influencing Congress went from 10,641 to 13,465 during the same 11 years period. That's a massive 26.5% (3) increase in lobbyists hovering around Washington and influencing how democracy is administered.

Reform of the tax code won't happen overnight according to Alice Rivlin, first CBO director under Clinton.

In early 2010 (4) this author put some pertinent questions to her on tax reform and practical solutions to the crisis looming, both fiscally and monetarily.

Ms. Rivlin's resume (5) is comprehensive including founding director of the CBO in 1975; director of Office of Management and Budget (1994-1996) during which she oversaw a balanced federal budget; and vice chair, Board of Governors of Federal Reserve System (1996-1999).

According to a study by Alan Auerbach and William Gale of U.C. Berkley (6) entitled "The Economic Crises and Fiscal Crisis: 2009 and Beyond" and presented the same day as the interview with Alice Rivlin, Federal Revenues as a percentage of GDP have gone from 5% in 1934 to between 22% and 16% during 2000 to 2008 period.

1. "A Brief Guide to the Flat Tax", by Daniel Mitchell, PhD.
http://www.heritage.org/Research/Taxes/bg1866.cfm
2. "Top 10 Heavy Hitters" List; "Industries: Accountants"
http://www.opensecrets.org/orgs/index.php
http://www.opensecrets.org/industries/indus.php?ind=F11
3. Total Lobbying Spending 1998-2009
http://www.opensecrets.org/lobby/index.php
4. Interview by phone January 15th 2010
5. Alice Rivlin: Biography – 1968-2003
http://www.brookings.edu/experts/r/rivlina.aspx
6. "The Economic Crises and Fiscal Crisis: 2009 and Beyond" by Auerbach and Gale
http://www.taxpolicycenter.org/events/events_011610.cfm

Taxes Collected

The IRS issues various reports on taxes collected, some timely, others three years off.

A recent example was IR-2009-17 (7), detailing taxes from 2006. In other words it takes the IRS two and half years to **report** on its collections. Usually when it wants to collect unreported income it is much more prompt.

In 2006, 138.4 million individuals filed. But 67% of these filers (93 million) were taxable. Total tax collected from this group was $1 trillion dollars, up 9.5% from 2005. As of 2010 March 3rd, there was no inkling of what had been collected from taxpayers in 2007.

Surely in this era of mega fast computers and the Internet, the IRS should be furnishing the people with timely information on taxes collected from individuals.

The main reason why the unemployment numbers are important for the government in general and the Treasury in particular has nothing to do with economic activity etc. but rather the tax take.

By projecting the unemployment rate, the tax take can be calculated accordingly. The more individuals employed the great the tax take and vice versa.

The BLS and Treasury work closely and ensure that statistics are promptly updated, ensuring an efficient counting of those employed and therefore eligible for tax collection.

As for relaying this information to the people no such urgency is needed.

According to the BLS, in February 2010, the total number of unemployed collecting benefits stood at 11.55 million. Remember this does not account for those who have given up searching for work and whose benefits have run out. If we look at BLS and use its numbers, 11.5 equates to about 10%, therefore the total labor market must be 115 million individuals.

If we look at those who have given up completely, then about 15% are well and truly without a job and either have run out of benefits or are still collecting.

Thus the real figure of those with no job is closer to 17.75 million people.

7. http://www.irs.gov/newsroom/article/0,,id=204956,00.html

Chapter 11

Modern Remit of the Fed

When a student of economics reads the chapter on the financial institutions and the FED in a conventional text book on macro-economics, monetary policy and the Federal Reserve Bank (FRB), a list of responsibilities are given: supervision of the banking system, maintenance of financial stability, lender of last resort and most importantly setting the interest rate charged to banks for overnight loans or fed funds rate.

In 2009, the FRB paid $46.1 billion in earnings to the Treasury [1]. According to the story it was the most ever paid "since the Fed started operating in 1914". And in 2009 the FRB "snapped up $300 billion in government debt" and bought "$1.25 trillion in mortgage backed securities from Fannie Mae and Freddy Mac".

To the casual reader this might sound like great news.

But on closer examination it is not.

First, where did the FRB get the money to "snap" up $300 billion?

Second, how can a bank that is a private entity buy mortgage backed securities on such a vast scale?

What is the guarantor of the FRB?

Answer 1. It printed the cash; 2. Purchased toxic assets with printed cash and; 3. The taxpayer.

Where in the FRB's charter was it given the authority to "snap up" government debt? And since it is not a government entity, isn't a vehicle for redistribution of wealth to other reckless banks, using the Treasury as the faucet or spigot? The US Treasury has in effect, become a distribution center of trades made by the FRB on behalf of reckless banks using the ever compliant and uninformed taxpayer as guarantor.

Then the mainstream media, in this case the AP writes a catchy headline pronouncing the Fed as savior of the system, giving vast billions to the Treasury that in turn gives it right back again to banks as TARP.

Recent intervention by the Fed involved a $16 Trillion extension of credit to the large banks in the United States at near zero rate of interest between 2008 and 2011.

In the 127 page GAO (2) report dated October 2011, entitled "Federal Reserve Bank Governance", widespread conflicts of interest were revealed involving several top executives using their influence as Fed directors to benefit their firms.

The famed CEO of JP Morgan Chase, Jamie Dimon also serves on the board of directors of the Federal Reserve Bank of New York and received near zero interest free loans for his bank at the height of the crisis.

Of 108 Federal Reverse board directors a whopping 82 were president of CEO of their company. And between 2006 and 2010, only 11 of the 202 experts in a variety of fields (including agriculture, commerce, industry, consumer interests and labor) represented the latter two: consumers and labor.

From this exhaustive GAO study one can presume that the Fed exists in the modern sense as a buffer for its member banks and NOT a manager of monetary policy and stabilization of prices (as is often assumed) for the public good.

What has happened over the past few years is a failure of the Fed to allow market forces to affect its biggest banking members i.e. Citigroup, JP Morgan et al.

Instead it has attempted to socialize losses and privatize profits, using the terror of financial Armageddon as a rallying call to the tax payer who is called to bail out reckless banks engaged in ultra-risky behavior.

This cannot go on into perpetuity as long as the ordinary Joe understands exactly what is going on.
A cursory look at who owns all of the US $14 Trillion in debt, shows that the single biggest owner of US debt is NOT China, Japan or any other foreign country but the FEDERAL RESERVE BANK itself!

According to the cable business news channel CNBC (3), owned by GE, of the outstanding $14 Trillion, the Fed and "intra-governmental holdings" owns about $5.35 Trillion. That's 38.2142857142857% (142857 recurring into infinity) of the total debt.

How do they get the money to buy the debt? Where does the money come from?

They print vast quantities and use accounting tricks to maneuver it into member bank accounts, and through the Treasury via IRS, tax the population into perpetuity.

It is worth noting that most if not all students of economics are lead to believe that a country's currency strength is based on a sound balance of trade and balance, in other words the more the country exports the better and the stronger its currency. A question that has to be posed having read all of the chapters of this book to date

1. *"Fed Paid Record $46.1 billion to Treasury Last Year", Associated Press*
http://finance.yahoo.com/news/Fed-paid-record-461B-to-apf-231123775.html?x=0
2. *http://sanders.senate.gov/imo/media/doc/d1218%20(2).pdf*
3. *http://www.cnbc.com/id/29880401/The_Biggest_Holders_of_US_Government_Debt*
March 25th 2009

Chapter 12

Prohibit Alcohol-Permit Income Tax

During the researching for and the writing of this book I was interested in the particular historical period 1913 to 1933, a twenty year span that saw huge changes in this country. World War I, the founding of the Fed, the beginnings of income tax, the genesis of government debt, the roaring twenties, the crash of '29, prohibition and the Great Depression.

Chronologically, income tax came before the founding of the Fed but replaced the liquor tax. In fact in the Anti-Saloon League (ASL) existed in the United States from 1893 until 1933, forty years of fighting against allowing the people to choose alcohol or temperance.

(1)   Poster: Anti-Liquor Poster circa 1919

Posters like the one above were used to terrify the population, born and unborn, about the demon drink and it effects. The ASL was a major lobbyist for the income tax and although between 67% and 70% of the federal government's revenue came from liquor before the passing of prohibition into the law of the land, the ASL pushed for the abolition of saloons, liquor and beer. The colossal blunder of the ASL and their prohibitionists was the destruction of jobs from carriage makers to haul the beer and liquor to barrel makers who made the containers that held the beer.

By destroying 500 breweries out of the 1000 per-prohibition, the ASL succeeded in degrading a sure and stable source of government revenue. These sources of revenue flowed from brewers, liquor makers, saloons and the legal sale of alcohol.

In 1920 for example federal revenue amounted to just $6.6 billion [*table (1) below*].

On page 25 of the 344 page document (1) – available online – the table shows a marked decrease in revenues collected after prohibition was implemented nationwide.

In 1923 only $3.8 billion had been collected. This as a result of the collapse of liquor and beer related sources. Now the burden would fall upon the worker who was to be taxed at ever increasing percentages as the system became more and more complex.

But by 1932 at the height of both prohibition and the Great Depression revenues had imploded to just $1.9 billion, a 50% decrease from nine years previously and a whopping 347% lower than the pre-prohibition era. By 1933 the repeal movement to reinstate the culture of drinking had gained momentum and in 1934 the federal government had collected more than $2.9 million in taxes.

Steadily the revenues collected increased and by 1942 they had reached a healthy $14.6 billion, 768% higher than the dark days of 1932.

Of course in 1942 America was at war. From then on deficits would be the new normal.

Year	Receipts (millions $)	Outlays (millions)	Surplus/Deficit (millions)
1919	5,130	18,493	-13,363 [WW I]
1920	6,649	6,358	291
1923	3,853	3,140	713
1932	1,924	4,659	-2,735
1934	2,955	6,541	-3,586
1942	14,634	35,137	-20,503
1952	66,167	67,686	-1,519
1992	1,091,328	1,381,649	-290,321
2012	3,075,328 (est.)	3,632,747	-557,419

Table (1) by Author

(1) Source: *Historical Tables Budget of the United States Government 2010*

During the Depression, income taxes had imploded because of the mass unemployment and there was no source coming from liquor and beer, unless the Mafia and Bootleggers paid up and that had the same probability as a snowball's chance in hell!

The key point to all these numbers is that two forces changed how the government would fund itself.

As the United States moved forward into the 1920s the collection of income taxation would act as a substitute for the prohibition era's banning on liquor, saloon and brewery taxes. Then as the flow of income taxes increased past the ninety fifties, the ability to borrow on the basis of taxation collected and military power became the new normal.

The national debt in 1961 stood at $290.6 billion (2). Fifty years later it stands at $14 trillion.

That's a 4817.8% increase in the nominal amount of the debt, even with adjustments for inflation this is a weapon of financial mass destruction given that total receipts for 2011 were estimated to bring in $3.614 trillion with a deficit of $929.4 billion.

The interest alone for the 2011 US national debt is the equivalent of the entire debt of 1961 or about $290 billion!

But at least we can buy alcohol with the weakened dollars we have in our pockets, wallets and bank accounts.

(1) http://www.gpoaccess.gov/usbudget/fy10/pdf/hist.pdf *Historical Tables Budget of the United States Government*

(2) *Treasury figures:* http://www.treasurydirect.gov/govt/reports/pd/histdebt/histdebt_histo4.htm

Conclusion

I began writing this short book after the financial crisis had been "averted", but something didn't seem right the more I read the conventional media reports during the "financial Armageddon".

As I researched and wrote the manuscript, I began to send a synopsis and sample chapters of the book to various publishers, all of whom did not want to publish the book, politely declining with the usual form letter or email.

Then it struck me why they would not take it on.

It was against the conventional wisdom on how the Fed operated and what it actually did in the economy.

We are living in a time of serious financial volatility. At the time of completion of this book Greece was about to call a referendum, Occupy Wall Street had spread across the length and breadth of the United States, banks were being lent money by the Fed at between 0% and .25% interest rate, while charging clients between 3 and 4.5% (1800% mark up!) on mortgages.

The Fed, by attempting to implement "Twist", QE-3 and other monetary tricks was ensuring that corporations and banks would continue to get cheap money, while bank customers who wished to save would get the shaft. During the period 2008 to 2010, the Fed had secretly lent $16,000,000,000,000 to member banks at near zero interest rate and only Bernie Sanders (I) from Vermont had the back bone to demand a more transparent audit of the Fed.

Eventually he got what he wanted in an exhaustive GAO report (mentioned in this book) on the Fed's conflicts of interest.

The Lame Stream Media (LSM) of course went without any reporting of this most important story.

Take a look at how much a dollar bill can buy today in 2011/2012.

When I arrived here in the late eighties I could get the following:

3 bagels for $1
1 pint of Guinness for $3
1 gallon of gasoline for $1.17 (New York State)
1 bedroomed apartment NYC for $850
1 semester tuition $900

In the intervening years the dollar has lost value against wheat, hops, oil, real estate accommodation and college education fees. As a result of this loss of value more of the currency has to be injected into the economy via credit cards, bank loans etc.

The Fed and its member banks are responsible for this massive credit and money bubble. When one of the member banks puts risky bets on exotic derivatives and loses the taxpayer is put on the hook.

On November 9th 2011, the US national debt is slated to hit $15,000,000,000,000, the majority of that will be owned by the Fed and its member banks.

The auction by Treasury will ensure that number is reached (see table below) and the debt game will continue on into 2012, regardless of Democrat or Republican in the White House!

Auction Announcement November 2nd 2011:

Announcement Date	Security Term	Security Type	CUSIP Number	Auction Date	Issue Date	Maturity Date
11-02-2011	3-YEAR	NOTE	912828RQ5	11-08-2011	11-15-2011	11-15-2014
11-02-2011	10-YEAR	NOTE	912828RR3	11-09-2011	11-15-2011	11-15-2021
11-02-2011	30-YEAR	BOND	912810QT8	11-10-2011	11-15-2011	11-15-2041
11-03-2011	91-DAY	BILL	9127953C3	11-07-2011	11-10-2011	02-09-2012
11-03-2011	182-DAY	BILL	9127955M9	11-07-2011	11-10-2011	05-10-2012

Source: Treasury Direct – http://www.treasurydirect.gov/RI/OFAnnce

The taxpayer will be required to repay the debt with interest while the Fed keeps buying up the Treasury issued debt into perpetuity.

The taxpayer will pay higher rates in taxes as interest rates in the future climb beyond the financial engineering the Fed has been attempting to implement through its "Twist", QE-1, and QE-2 and anticipated QE-3.

The dollar we have in our pockets will be worth less and less as the money supply saturates the economy over the next few years.

Finally there will be an end point to all of this. It will start with ordinary people waking up and seeing the Fed for what it really is – a private institution that has gone way beyond its mandate over the past 98 years.

November 11, 2011